Praise for
Do Unto Earth

"A must-read book for everyone who cares about the future of humanity and our planet."

—**Dr. Ervin Laszlo**, two-time Nobel Peace Prize nominee, recipient of the Goi Peace Prize and International Mandir of Peace Prize, best-selling author of Science and the Akashic Field, founder of the Laszlo Institute of New Paradigm Research and The Club of Budapest, fellow of the World Academy of Art and Science and the International Academy of Philosophy of Science

"A 911 call from Planet Earth herself, *Do Unto Earth* is a potent manifesto for living life today and forward. This book should be required reading in schools. We must act now!"

—**Mary Madeiras**, three-time Emmy-Winning director, screenwriter, Akashic Records practitioner, activist, and author

"*Do Unto Earth* is full of empowering messages and mind-bending assertions that you won't find in science or history textbooks. Given the urgent need for new solutions on this endangered planet, the ideas are worthy of further investigation."

—**Mark Gober**, author of *An End to Upside Down Thinking*, board of directors of the Institute of Noetic Sciences (IONS) and the School of Wholeness and Enlightenment (SoWE)

"From page one, I was hooked! *Do Unto Earth* merges spirituality with our environmental crisis and does it in a way that is as gripping as a blockbuster movie. Brava to Hayes, Borgens … and Pax."

—**Temple Hayes**, author, spiritual leader, animal activist, and founder of illli.org

"The channeled Spirit energy Pax states that we are at the 'crossroads of our survival' and offers us bold envisioning and direction. Mother Earth is speaking, and ancient mysteries are revealed! Let's heed and implement these game-changers for the benefit of us all."

—**Sunny Chayes**, social/human rights and environmental activist, feature writer and Chief Strategic Partner for Whole Life Times, and host of ABC's *Solutionary Sundays*

"Timely, high-level and generative wisdom detailing how we may still sustain our beautiful planet while reclaiming our collective and individual sovereignty."

—**Stephan McGuire**, director of Zürich-based NGO Cernunnos Media, Director of Tree Media Foundation

Pax and the Path of Purpose

Pax and the Path of Purpose

Volume 5 of Do Unto Earth

PENELOPE JEAN HAYES,
CAROLE SERENE BORGENS

Waterside Productions

Cover design by:
Andrew Green
Books & Illustration

Printed in the United States of America

First Printing, 2020

ISBN-13: 978-1-947637-63-4 print edition
ISBN-13: 978-1-951805-00-5 ebook edition

Waterside Productions
2055 Oxford Ave
Cardiff, CA 92007
www.waterside.com

For you—
so you know for certain that you are the change and
you have the power

Contents

Introduction

*D*o *Unto Earth* is an extraordinary conversation intended to quantum leap us forward in our spiritual evolution and journey to enlightenment. This message is not a directive delivered from a thousand feet up; this is a very personal message from and dialogue with the Divine Wisdom Source directly to you and for you. Please accept this gift with eyes clear and wide and open.

Within these pages is the blueprint for environmental repair and peace and unity on Earth, however, this booklet constitutes just one of eight volumes that together make up that blueprint. While we believe that the eight topics, as separated by these volumes, are to be understood as connected to each other and only together give the full message as intended, we also understand some readers prefer to focus on their specific areas of interest—hence these eight mini-books by volumes. (Note: Chapters within this volume are numbered as they originally appeared in the book's full-length version.)

As you begin this journey, you might like to know how this collaboration of writing began.

It is indeed my great joy and honor to communicate with the Spirit Messenger, Pax, channeled by Carole Serene Borgens. From a young age, Carole, a former nurse, diligently studied all things metaphysical. This Spirit Messenger first visited her in the early 1990s when she was new to channeling by automatic writing. When her pen wrote the opening introduction and request for her to be a channel, she recognized the profound responsibility attached and jumped up from her office chair to pace the floor—not easy with three sleeping Irish Wolfhounds covering the carpet. Carole's initial response was to ask if she could think about it and take some time to respond, which she was given. Asking, "Why me?" Spirit responded to her: "You are new to this, you have no bad habits, and you will change none of my words." In time, Carole came to be comfortable with this blessing and so began her journey.

I, too, have been a seeker and spiritualist since my years as a teenaged runaway, and so it is a useful tool at times for me to reach out to a reputable intuitive for deeper guidance. Beginning on the fourth of February 2019, I had several long-distance Spirit channeling sessions with Carole—she was in British Columbia and I was in Florida. I had copious questions for Spirit as I sought further direction for my second title, *Do Unto Earth* (which, incidentally, is also the name of my business), while building upon the message of my first title, *The Magic of Viral Energy*. I was expanding and broadening the message of "viral energy" from personal and interpersonal goals to global concerns facing humanity and Planet Earth. I was also simultaneously establishing the Viral Energy Institute, a learning and research platform for the study of Viralenology.

Through our talks, this Spirit Messenger and I were getting to know each other and Spirit felt my passion for the plight of abused animals and species extinction, as well as my intention to bring awareness to our environmental crisis and to share the impacts of "viral energy masses"—large energetic fields created by both light and heavy intentions and action by communities, populations, industries, governments, and cultural beliefs—on Planet Earth. These disruptive energy masses create massive vibrational pockets of particular energies including love, hate, peace, discord, gratitude, violence, forgiveness, indifference, and compassion.

The Spirit Messenger seemed very interested in this direction and before long, Carole contacted me to say that Spirit wished to offer wisdom to be used by and shared through the Viral Energy Institute regarding this mission of planetary healing.

The writing began on the second of October 2019 when I sent questions to Carole who then channeled Spirit's responses by automatic writing (today, she does this via typing). It was *during* the writing that it became clear to all that this conversation would take book form and adopt the title *Do Unto Earth*.

As the answers were returned from Spirit, Carole and I both had many moments of excitement and more than a few gasps followed by, "Ooooh crikey, this is going to change everything!" The first of such revelations came in Chapter One when I asked the Spirit Messenger (whom self-identified with the moniker

"**Pax**", meaning peace) to be more specific about who they are. Here was the answer...

> "**We are one with the Universe, not the Universe alone. We are the Divine Universe, yes, and the God being and the greater wisdom, that which knows and supports all and is healing, non-judgmental and tolerant, all-seeing, all-knowing, and Peace.**"

Volume 5

Do Unto Earth
Pax and the Path of Purpose

"*I recently watched an interview with the astronauts who, back in 1968, took the iconic photo that's come to be called 'Earthrise'. I marveled at the ecstatic joy they must have felt at their first sighting of our blue home suspended in the vast, dark firmament. How small we must have appeared. How fragile our existence. How enormous our potential.*"

Oprah Winfrey
American TV host, actress, producer,
and world-renowned spiritualist

Chapter Thirteen

The Life of Life

*P*ax, today it feels to me like I just watched an electrifying movie and at the very end, the next sequel was revealed. Now I get to watch the story unfold and I'm grateful and committed to this next destination of our journey together.

As we get going, I'd like to ask you a number of questions that have long interested humankind. When I looked up "Questions You Would Ask God", these were among the top queries; curiosities that are shared by many people. Here goes—

Why does light always win over darkness? How is this a certainty?

You may shine a light into darkness and it will illuminate what is there, previously unseen before arrival of the light. Darkness will not extinguish light in the context of this discussion. As more of your people become light-workers, the balance tips in favor of goodness and wellness for your planet. These are the new breed of scientists plus many more of your Earth people learning they can make a difference and will be part of the solution now.

Why do bad things happen to good people?

Who is to say what is a bad thing for another? When there is not a way of knowing what that person's life blueprint is, there is not a way to determine for them if an occurrence is a bad thing or a good thing. Remember this.

Why do bad people often get their way?

Is a "bad person" a ramification of what others deemed good people did not say or do when they should, a result of others' lack of forward motion in manifesting what should be, according to them? Is it lack of empowerment, weakness, or just a lesser amount of corruption?

When what is deemed bad by some is met with a sufficient amount of good, as deemed by those same people, physics would have it that there is an impasse. Do you understand this lesson? The simplicity of it is that without resistance, whatever pushes forward continues in motion.

Yes, I do understand this.
Many people want to know why the Spirit World won't step in and stop suffering caused by cruel or greedy people. Why is suffering _allowed_?

That people wish to hand over responsibility for your current world situation to the Spirit World indicates a lack of willingness to accept your role in creating this world situation. Do not consider your creation of a mess is the responsibility of others to fix.

We ask your world population to understand there are consequences to your actions—*an action has a reaction*—and yours is to repair the damage you have actively caused or passively allowed to be. It is yours to undertake the next chapter in this story.

This, of course, is reasonable—that we clean up our own mess.

Let's look at this question about suffering, not as related to our environmental crisis, but as related to historical atrocities such as the Holocaust. There were millions of people praying for a divine intervention—praying for years, even—and in the end, some six million Jews were murdered by the Nazis. That being said, I hope that this is a fair question: why could the Spirit World not intervene to help?

The division between chosen directions by those on Earth and those not is the answer. One does not interfere in the other.

That world powers initiated an action is for it to play out in history. There does not seem to be a reason but in fact the reason is there.

For your history to show the steps along the way from beginning to end of this you refer to is to put in place the example for the world to follow going forward—what to see and experience that teaches the reasons for avoidance in future.

We see this is currently underway again and being watched *but not disallowed by your population.*

An example was set in this that took many lives and this example is to teach the future.

As it is being elevated now in memory, it is to have a resurgence of emotion among your people and reintroduce and rekindle the will to *not* accept this in future.

It is happening—be watchful.

Oh Pax, please do tell us more regarding this clear warning.

In the world today, sadly we are largely bystanders of many acts of extreme wickedness in many countries, including but not limited to the mistreatment and mutilation of women in some religions; the crisis of "ethnic cleansing" genocide of the Muslim Rohingya people in northwestern Myanmar; the civil war in South Sudan with its brutal killings and rapes; the deadly conflicts in the Central African Republic between the Christian militias called the "anti-Balaka" and Muslim groups, rising to a level of genocide; and atrocities by Arab militias against non-Arab peoples in Darfur, a region in western Sudan.

Much of the genocide occurring in present times is taking place in African countries, and like the Holocaust these are the outcomes of religious and ethnic divides and hatred.

I must mention one of the biggest and most profitable criminal businesses in the world that is also one of the most prolific and yet little-known (or little discussed) horrors: human sex trafficking and the global sex trade, and the fact that at this very moment there are more than four million adults and one million children in forced sexual slavery worldwide.

Of these and other acts of barbarity, to what do you refer when you speak of the Holocaust in warning us that "this is currently underway again", and "it is happening"? Which of these many horrors do you see escalating to the level of the Holocaust?

We speak of divisiveness among populations and individuals by race, color, religion, gender, anywhere there can be one group of peoples denying another equality. This is the Holocaust reference and how that began.

It is underway now among some races and countries and they deny equality to those who do not look like them—a resurgence of the Aryan Race *mindset* extended throughout your global societies. This is as dangerous as it ever was, and more so now in your age of electronic communication where misinformation spreads in nanoseconds.

Please use the example of the Holocaust to help us understand that "light always wins over darkness".

When people take positive action against what they see as negative, it is light over darkness.

That nobody stood up then to disrupt the negative movement allowed darkness to rule.

It was not that light was lost or failed; it was that light was not shown to the dark.

Inaction and blind following without question was the cause.

What is the true nature of mankind? Are we good or bad by nature?

Consider the nature of a baby at birth, a child growing; innocence is the true nature. This is what begins, what is intrinsically yours: purity of intention.

It is what is taught, what is learned that makes the change. Is racism intrinsic to the baby, is greed and a tendency to corruption, is cheating and bullying a part of the baby, or is it learned behavior? You decide.

What caused us to move away from our true nature?

Influence. Influence of those in control of life and commerce and learning and building and growing relationships—these account for change, these influence change.

What must happen to allow a child to grow into maturity without these influences taking over? Self-empowerment and confidence and trust in self—these are the needed barriers to the destruction of purity of spirit. Is it the case that these are also learned behaviors? Is it more to the point that these attributes are within each person at birth and are lost as the child grows in experience? Yes. This is it. Each person does not learn these traits, each person is born with them and either retains or loses them based on nurture. Parents and the "nature versus nurture" aspect of humanity will determine if the child becomes an adult with confidence, compassion, empathy, good humor, forgiveness, strong work ethic, and an abundance of care and concern for all nature and mankind. These are all found within the individual's DNA and are either lost or retained as life progresses. The soul arrives in purity.

Does the Universe operate only by physics or does it "think", make choices, and so on?

It is our joy to share what is of benefit to your Earth people. From time to time we must ask that you accept what is without the minutia of understanding that comes from dissection such as this. While philosophical in nature, the thought is a psychological one of contradiction and comparison.

In this case there are secrets to be uncovered, mysteries to be explored and grand information to be known and tested. Life goes on and the world takes many turns while awaiting this series of events. For now, it is fair to say that when your space exploration is taking place this too shall be further explored.

We suggest that the understanding of all things heretofore left to imagination is to continue while your mankind works out the implications of trying to manage their own lives on your planet. With your present inability to do so, more attention could be paid to the peace on Earth policy and the love thy neighbor policy and the true nature of mankind-coming-to-the-fore policy.

It is time now for your people to look within for their peace and use this time to reflect on what is and what could be. Managing life on your Earth has not gone well of late, and it is time to turn your efforts in this direction.

This is true.
What's the purpose of a person's life?

What is each soul's purpose as laid out long ago and agreed to on each go around?

For some the meaning of life is to gain control and financial wealth, yet for others it is to heighten their spiritual wellness and strength of character, to teach the ways of the Higher Self—never the twain shall meet, but there are myriads of meanings in between. To each his own it is.

At that soul's inception is the blueprint determined for each life's purpose. This is a contract between the Universe and the soul to guide the way to future growth and wisdom, wellness, and greater movement toward enlightenment.

Between physical incarnations is there a processing of our life and a process for preparing for the next incarnation?

This determination is made by each soul considering return, and is the continuation of their journey toward enlightenment, toward completion of their blueprint for life and lifetimes. There are journeys to take resulting in contributions to global wellness or following the course of one life to ensure it is on track to wellness, and amazing gifts to share and experiences as well. To regroup in the Spirit realm prior to return includes the choices and the preparations for what is to come. Some wish immediate return and do so by choosing to be an unborn baby in their family, returning that way to bring love again to the circle. Others have much healing, both physical and emotional, to manage before considering their next adventure on your Earth—it varies.

It sounds like a soul comes back fairly quickly after death, that is if they don't have much healing to undertake between lifetimes. How thrilling that we could bump into a loved one or know them again in another incarnation. Is it *common* for

a deceased loved one's soul to reenter the physical plane at the same time that we're still here?

It is not uncommon and is dependent entirely upon the lessons remaining to be taught and to be learned. It is a possibility and results in healing by way of those remaining becoming aware of the new soul in their midst having remarkable abilities to trigger feelings and memories and healing. Always there is a higher purpose.

Is the choosing of a "life purpose" a formal event, like a meeting in the Spirit realm?

The Universe celebrates all growth toward enlightenment. However, as the soul's progress is dependent on its own timetable through its development, the transition is a personal one.

Life is a choice, don't you know?

Does this mean that *everything* in life is a choice?

Indeed, it is, beginning with choice of parents to enter the next lifetime and everything throughout that lifetime. What comes will come, and how it is reacted to is your choice. Think on it—each time you make a decision to go or do it has been a choice.

If an illness is presented, how it is reacted to and therefore the outcome is a choice. To accept or reject the realities of life influences outcomes, and each decision along that path is a choice.

Free will equals choice, and those with limited free will choose to be compliant or not. All choices, and those with choice are empowered to control outcomes.

What about terminal diseases—if a person had terminal cancer, can they choose their way out of it to health?

Choice began with the acquisition of the disease as a component of the chosen life blueprint. Remember this.

Do we choose our death?

The blueprint for life that one creates for themselves and their next incarnation includes the ending of that lifetime.

All is a choice, yes, and pertains to the lessons intended to be learned and taught and shared. It is the contract one makes with one's self and the Universe for that period in time; their presence at that place in time.

Death is a beginning of the next chapter in a soul's progress, the next lessons in a next incarnation. It is a process—a soul's journey.

Is there a time when it's too late for choice?

Once the contract has been made, we say it is, it becomes the way forward. There is this trajectory of life that is patterned according to the chosen steps along the path for the lifetime.

A person capable of changing that trajectory is a rare one and would require much personal work to determine why the path was chosen, what was to be learned from it, and why a deviation would be appropriate. Regarding the pertinent past lifetime, to recognize the signposts for this journey would be needed along with forgiveness and openness to acceptance of the what and why of it.

Regarding karma, do we keep coming back until we "get it right" or learn a lesson? Or, perhaps there are no "lessons", there is just what we choose to create?

Karma—this is an interesting discussion, as it is known by other names in other realms. What is the common thread is the action of it, the magnetic pull to continue a lesson or right a wrong or contribute what was withheld and so many opportunities lost are wanting to be revisited and rectified.

It is a self-imposed state of being and is very real.

Pain is caused by lost opportunities and it is the way-of-correcting that exists in order to not only do right but create peace within the self that is needing release from the wishing for other outcomes. It is a process and a valuable set of lessons and repeating with new knowledge and clear intention to contribute good where it was previously lacking. It is a blessing to all.

Apart from finding a good hypnotherapist for past life regression, is there a way to review a past life that is helpful to a current lifetime?

We wish to state that there is a difference between past life regression and hypnosis therapy. One can take place without the other.

Meditation does it for many, so consider the deep and guided meditation which takes one through the process of reviewing life and lifetimes with the intention to visit the one pertinent to present life blocks or challenges. This can be managed at home through the use of guided meditation recordings. It is effective and can be therapeutic and liberating.

Is it possible to reach a level of "consciousness attainment" while in the physical, whereby a soul decides to (or graduates to) remain purely spirit?

Remaining in pure spirit is a choice made on the other side. There are those souls who do so, preferring to remain to welcome and to teach and to communicate as we do as guides. Stages and processes and passages of time determine who is what and where, and the why is determined by each.

I'd like to talk about our transition between all of these lifetimes that our soul experiences.

My dad had a near-death experience many years ago. He described floating at the ceiling of the room and looking down on his limp body in the hospital bed. He then said that a tunnel opened above, and it had walls of gaseous grey clouds that were slowly turning like a vortex. At the end of the tunnel, far ahead, he could see a doorway emitting brilliant yellow-white light—an actual doorway.

What is this experience all about? Why a tunnel? Why a doorway at the end?

Each person sees their own version of the way to their heaven. It is not a universal vision except that there is a bright and welcoming light. The doorway, of course, is a universal recognition of an option, another dimension behind the door perhaps, and if you choose to open the door, another place to be.

Oh, so these are symbols, compelling for each person and for all. And, what is "the light" at the end of the tunnel?

The light is the welcoming arms of those loved ones who have gone before and are now present to greet them when moving from body into spirit. It is love energy to envelope them while transitioning into spirit.

Your people must recognize that the common denominator in these near-death experiences is that there is another place to be, and that heavenly place, as described by many, is in the light that draws them forward. It is where they will be welcomed and brought into spirit, if they choose to make that journey. If they are not yet ready, they will return to the body but retain the feelings and visions of that magnetic light which is filled with love and acceptance.

That's a peaceful and comforting vision.

Many people live their lives as if getting "*there*" is the goal: the ultimate achievement to arrive in the Afterlife with an unscathed soul and to, at last, relax in that place of eternal rest and peace. As if holding their breath for the finish line, many believe that "Heaven" is the reward and goal, and the whole point of making it through a grueling physical lifetime. Yet, if it were indeed a *choice* to return to physical, why wouldn't every soul choose to stay in spirit form in the Spirit World?

It is the message of much organized religion that life is to be lived in excruciating purity in order to enter the gates of heaven, or known by other names—the final reward. It is the journey that is as important, if not more, and to be considered its own reward.

To remain, between incarnations, in spirit form is to deny the continuation of life with family and friend groupings chosen to re-enter for purposes of completing cycles of transformation within those groups. Continuation and finalization is important, returning to teach and to learn through a choice of parents and family groups is what many long for. To learn what more can be gained through human form that can contribute to the overall wellbeing of humankind, it spreads beyond small family thinking and toward global change.

It is our wish that your people understand that they have unlimited potential on your world stage. We do not see this as a widely understood innate ability and it is our wish to inform now that to each there is a season, a reason, and a lifetime to become what is in each heart.

We have *unlimited* potential in our world? Through your last passage, I'm getting the impression that the physical dimension is not a test or penance or a hardship—as some might think—but rather, it's an opportunity and a sought-after adventure and the "stage" where growth and spiritual evolution plays out.

While we are in-between lifetimes, are we fully empowered in our potential before we re-enter the next physical incarnation? And if so, when and why do we forget that we have unlimited potential?

Not always—there is healing to be done, as stated above.

Unlimited potential and the having of it—is it forgotten or is it not instilled in children as they grow? And for some it is denied or scoffed at or simply not supported by parents as an option. For those downtrodden *themselves* it often is not a concept that their children can overtake their accomplishments and proceed through life with a positive attitude while accomplishing their goals.

There is a choice of parents that will or will not support the spirit in its relocation into a lifetime and the level of challenge it will encounter in trying for heightened wellbeing. It is a crapshoot at times, and at others, well planned.

Well, well: I am surprised to hear that a soul's next lifetime can be a "crapshoot" and not always well planned. I mean, come on, a soul can be in an Earth lifetime for many decades; wouldn't anyone want to plan such an adventure (at the very least to plan out the inborn circumstances that will aid the soul's purpose and spiritual evolution)? Why are some lifetimes given less planning consideration?

You must understand this is entirely dependent upon that soul's choice. Lifetimes are determined to provide opportunity to teach and to learn as well as to reconnect with known relatives for continuation of a journey. This is one factor, another is to arrive as soon as possible to jump in once again to Planet Earth and join a movement, such as climate change, with the intent to make a difference and improvement. The chosen parents or family is not the key ingredient in the decision, and as a result could go either way in terms of support. Understand that differing motivations result in differing pathways—it is the way of it.

Do souls ever choose to return in the next lifetime to a different planet and peoples other than Earth?

An interesting consideration this is. Our suggestion is that souls may return to Planet Earth civilization or remain in spirit for brief or long periods of time. To decide to shoot away to another unknown life journey is not the way.

We do not say this will continue as the norm as changes in Earth people's lifestyles come, as interstellar travel by Earth people becomes regular, and as what is to be found is found and changes the way of your living; all things are changeable.

What is to be found is the ability to relocate and travel and these options are presented as available to those open to this change and challenge. It will form a part of the journey to the next age of your people.

Pax, if we didn't have stress, guilt, regret energy, and environmental pollution, how long could the human body last? How long do we have the *potential* to live?

Think of clean air and water, clean food and clean thinking and living without angst? A century or more would be quite *average* without the body growing unwell. This time may come again. It is a far journey, however, from present day world situations to a place of purity and longevity. All is possible—you should begin the journey. Trust in yourselves to know the way.

May you please give us a succinct sentence or two of what life is like in the Spirit realm for those souls who have crossed over?

Loving, learning, teaching, support, growth, return, release, joy, welcoming, progress toward the next journey. Love is the over-riding sense of being in this place on the journey: a jumping-off point for the next lessons.

I have so many questions for you. Like—where do our pets go when they die?

Your Earth people have an understanding that the Rainbow Bridge is the place of gathering their souls while they await the arrival of their earthly guardians when they pass over.

Personally, I'd rather think that my sweet kitty, Sabrina, who died at twenty-three-years-old would come back as another pet in my life. I don't like the idea of her waiting for me, especially if my soul decided to rather expeditiously come right back to physicality. Is there another scenario of our pets reincarnating and living again in our current lifetime?

Be aware that this time at the Rainbow Bridge is filled with happiness and play, enjoyment of youthful activities.

Your choice to return quickly or not is not a major concern as there is no linear time to be felt and when you realize this it changes all.

In the blink of an eye many lifetimes on Earth have come and gone while the pets play on.

Does the animal soul *evolve* through lifetime incarnations as people do?

This is a question not often addressed, and it is the case that it can be.

Do we make agreements with our pets as to how our souls will journey together?

That you may journey again together is a choice, an agreement that may be fulfilled with a meeting elsewhere in time of spirits.

Where do other animals such as farmed animals go when they die?

There is a need for peace and harmony for them, as some have not enjoyed that in life, and this is a consideration as their final chapter on the Earth plane.

Do farmed animals of any kind reincarnate?

It is based on a willingness of that animal and does not seem to be the norm, as stated above.

Let's say that it is their final chapter as a cow or a chicken, for instance: where does that soul go after physical death? Do they get to now enjoy the peace and love of the Spirit World?

In the pastures of peace, indeed.

The term "Spirit Animal" has been used by First Nations and indigenous people to indicate that they feel a connection to and bolster energy or powers from a certain animal or species of wildlife. Is there such thing as a Spirit Animal and is there a sharing of strength, traits, or powers between a Spirit Animal and a person?

Most certainly and it is recorded in the history of your people. It is the spirit of the animal that holds the strength, the power, and results in many people trying to emulate the powers of their chosen animal spirit. To do so brings enhanced abilities both physical and spiritual.

Chapter Fourteen

Tap Your Cell Memory

*P*ax, we have much to explore in understanding our innate abilities. To go deeper, may you please explain cell memory?

While the mind gives many signs and signals also, it is the Higher Self involvement of the soul memory that brings knowledge, information, and guidance in nanoseconds and tiny particles that combine to form a picture of what is to be, in feeling or knowing or vision—either way it is a protection to be acknowledged.

I'd like to understand the "tiny particles" that you speak of in this context.

Oh yes, this is the information highway of the Higher Self advising the self, the body, and the mind of information needed to proceed in safety. It is the knowingness that comes with experience and memory—cell memory. It is to be recognized as such and acknowledged and attention paid, as it is the early warning system in operation.

Not all benefit from this Oversoul of care—to be blessed by your knowing of its presence—for your well-being and protection.

What is the "Oversoul"?

We have said that this Oversoul is your Higher Self consciousness sum total of past lifetime experiences on which to draw for current day information needs. Your link to this wisdom is within you, of course, and is accessed through your inner wisdom search engines (this is to resonate with the youth) and with your asking to connect.

You have the wisdom of the ages coursing through you, in your soul, which has traveled with you through many lifetimes and carries the wisdom and experiences of all of your lifetimes. Through accessing your memory banks, you can learn and grow and understand, and grow into the wise individual you have the power to be.

To not acknowledge these cell memories that affect your lives in positive and negative ways is to disallow the growth from knowledge of what has gone before; who and where you have been and the strengths and challenges you bring to your current lifetime. These are to grow with and understand they will elevate you to the place of understanding your lessons in this Earth school, this time around.

To recognize the lessons is step one, to follow your plotted course of learning is next, and to be open to following this path guarantees the process is to flow well for you. Remain open and watch for the signposts along the way. The rainbow brings the opening of the gate and the clouds will line the trail.

You have a golden highway on which to travel from your place of asking to your place of touching down in the knowledge/energy storage vault. Anyone can access this place within their Higher Self—it is there and awaits.

Is "the rainbow brings the opening of the gate" mere beautiful imagery or is this a real thing that you can tell me about?

We say the "rainbow" represents increased awareness and trust in oneself.

As in your world, a rainbow is reportedly to show the place of a pot of gold at its end, this we say identifies the time and place of growth in spirituality to the extent that it can be equated to finding gold.

Clouds lining the trail represent a tangible feel of walls defining the path for each of you, and their somewhat solid composition ensures you do not step off your path when you recognize the difference between the positive of the rainbow and the potential of negative in the clouds. Roadmaps they are, and quite recognizable for their guidance we say.

Very nice—thank you.

Are there a finite number of souls in the Universe and those souls just keep getting reincarnated? Or, are brand new souls created? And if so, from where do brand new souls come? And, if new souls are created, does it follow that some souls cease to exist, or is creation just a matter of more and more, such as exponential growth? (*Whew!*)

Ah well now, this is the question of the ages and those souls continuing to travel through the ages are the dear ones to us. As experience and knowledge grows and is shared, the wonder of it all expands and grows also. There are new beginnings and there are endings, and each has its place. As a soul's journey completes there is a diminishing number and as a new sprouting comes there is an increase. How does the new soul sprout, you ask? It is *seeded* and occupies a place for which it is destined. The seeding is the wisdom of the ages presenting the next step in a journey for worlds involved and people involved and becomes a new beginning from which grows progress and continued evolution of the process.

We have a long-standing philosophy that says that energy cannot be created or destroyed. Given that souls have "beginnings" and "endings", it would seem to me that energy is indeed created, and energy is indeed destroyed. What do you say?

Energy is shifted and warped and stretched and twisted and expanded and contracted and occasionally hidden, although it remains a presence. There is never only one way in the Universe. It dissipates and flares and becomes all-encompassing while diminishing to a candle flame—it will not be defined as one way.

What is causing the Universe to *exponentially* expand—more and more and faster and faster in its expansion?

Energy: internal and planetary at the core, energy. This continues movement as it shows itself and will continue as the fire within the core of your planet continues to burn. This creates energy which must be accommodated, and as you magnify the core of your planet by the number of others in existence, the energy must go somewhere, yes? To occupy the existing space was the idea, and as growth reaches the edges of that space, something must change, or catastrophic ends come to what is within. To pre-empt that, space expands to match. There is an expression about "expanding to fill the available space." Where you think that came from?

You are saying that the creation of more energy causes the Universe to expand. Therefore, energy *can* most definitely be created, and it is. This is extraordinary information, especially since our scientists do not know why the Universe is

exponentially expanding. It expands from within all areas (not only from the point called the Big Bang). In fact, the outer reaches of the Universe expand even more rapidly than sectors of galaxies that are already fully developed—which makes sense with what you're telling us because expansion occurs as new creation happens.

To be sure, is this recap accurate?

Indeed, it is accurate—would we tell you a story?

There is much to know and grow within your science, and we contemplate the outer edges of reality as the place where some seekers like to spend time. Others who look for basic and intellectually understandable and provable theories are missing the opportunity to step out of their comfort zones and explore the ethers—herein lie the answers.

Out of our comfort zone and into the ethers: I like that.

It is curious for most that our cells hold the memories of all of our past lifetimes and the wisdom of the ages. Being that we're speaking about memory, is it just the cells of our *brain* that hold this "cell memory"?

Oh ho, not so we say. The repository for cell memory is *all* cells.

How can we access this cell memory, and, well, *remember* it?

This is not the way of it to remember all as it would be detrimental given there are negative as well as positive cell memories.

As the need arises to remember reasons why an emotional challenge, for example, needs understanding, it is accomplished through accessing one's Higher Self in going within. Some meditate, some use other means, but accessing one's inner wisdom and knowing is the way.

If the "coding" of all memory is held *in our cells*—as opposed to in our minds—then is it possible for scientists to find this memory-content within our cells: to see this movie of soul memories and wisdom? Basically, can it be measured or found by science?

As long as science remains far removed from spirituality there is little likelihood of this meeting. There is no measurement available now for this esoteric substance.

All right, all of our cells hold all of the memories of all of our past lifetimes. This is quite a library of wisdom for those who learn to access it.

Does our cell memory also contain wisdom that might benefit us in terms of healthcare and the possibility of new medical exploration?

As you know, a salamander can grow a new tail when needed, as the body remembers what was there before and recreates it. Isn't that a thought that can bring science to a place of growing new organs and limbs on the human body, as needed? Science is, in fact, addressing this need now, and in laboratories around the globe are fascinating discoveries being made on how to sequence nerves to instruct the body to do the very thing: grow a new arm or leg, finger or liver.

It is a matter of time only.

I am against testing on animals, and so may you please explain a method that we can use for experimentation to make this discovery *without* using animals?

In your now the "need" for answers for humanity precludes the wish to not include animal testing.

Pax, I'm empowered in my purpose and one of my roles is as a vocal protector of animals, and so I feel that I can say to you that I cannot accept that answer; not even from you.

The reason is that many humans are so selfish and devolved in consciousness that they test on animals in the most torturous and heinous ways. This statement from you (without crystal clear clarification) can be misinterpreted by the many who have no respect for the lives and pain of animals, and who would only use such medical miracles to monetize a product or process while having zero concern for animal suffering. Please

keep in mind that, upon hearing this information, some humans would proceed to cut off the arm of a fully conscious chimpanzee, cat, or dog just to see if it grows back, and then they would study the tortured animal to determine why the limb didn't regenerate.

It is time to think outside the box in terms of experimenting—if it breathes, it should not be subjected to laboratory testing.

I'm glad you made that clear. Can we find an alternate suggestion then, please?

Here's one: I live in southern Florida. I see salamanders every day and they're not hard to catch (ask our cats, Max and Andy, who find lizards daily while playing in our screened lanai) and yes, if the salamander loses its tail, it can break free and carry on with its life, unharmed. Can our scientists catch only salamander tails and then release the animal to freedom? Would that be sufficient to test on? Or, can you gift us with the knowledge of a future method?

In medical science today there is a diminishing appetite for animals in labs. There are other ways being defined now with DNA sharing and 3D printing and you know science has these means to adapt.

Three-dimensional printing? This is a mind-expanding moment for me. Are you saying that

an organ, body part, or an entire body model can be 3D printed, and if so, that truly efficacious medical testing can be done on a dummy-human?

Indeed, this is the case and underway in your science. While it appears now that this is in the initial stages, behind the scenes are experiments on the printing side of development which are awe inspiring and bring your Earth people close to the ways of your off-planet cousins. They, of course, can clone and recreate a body almost at will—it is old school there. You have far to go on this journey, Caterpillar. (But yours is the right track).

That the world needs to take a few turns before much more is unveiled is a good thing—we think those who read these words and are involved will understand their need to rise above greed and corruption and protect these developments for the betterment of mankind, both physically and philosophically. We leave this discussion for your consideration.

We marvel at the tenacity of your scientists to find the way, as they will, and integrity must be top of mind here as this is serious business, this "cloning" of humans, which is to come in a mainstream manner.

At this time, making a salamander tail or a human organ is a given. So much more to come to benefit mankind—we should like to see that the developments soon to be unveiled are intended as a benefit and not to monetize a finding of science.

Well, yes, as I'm sure a new human organ would fetch quite a price from those who can afford it.

And, I can't let your mention of *alien* cloning slip by. I'd like to better understand the concept of cloning and see if we can share some moral guidelines, if you will. When ETs clone a body to harvest new body organs and parts, would the clone not have a soul of its own?

A reminder that the cloning of a body is not for the purpose of harvesting organs—there is no need for this as organs are created at will and require no bodily host.

It is the case that pieces and parts are made as needed and there isn't a container with soul involved. It's much more simple and not philosophical in nature that this practice exists. It has become the norm in advanced society where advances are such that your worldly practices appear primitive.

There is no moral component, as you ask; it is a matter of repair and replacement parts, much like your automobiles. That is all.

Then, if organs and parts can grow back, what is the use of the cloning of an alien being?

Cloning is for particular purposes involving new models, much like your automobiles where updated features are researched and then developed. There is always a purpose.

Like what? What's an example of a purpose for cloning?

A purpose would be to introduce a feature allowing for developments aimed at the greater good for all. Off-planet ideas and ideals and the continuation of community in the big picture—there are reasons which in time will be known.

Chapter Fifteen
The Power Within

*M*any years ago, I watched a movie called *The Power of One* (1992). It's a film about a boy in South Africa who positively changed the life of an entire village. Like the title of the movie suggests, the message was that one person can make a difference, and this ideal made an impression on me from a young age.

As a result of practicing my impact and the power of my intentions, I do believe that I can make a different in the world, and that each and every person can do so, too: we just have to have the intention, and then act.

We are here with you today, Penelope, for those people who need a nudge in the direction of understanding their own abilities and acting upon the knowledge that they are powerful—if they believe they are—and able to accomplish all that they dream of.

We have seen the best and now we see the worst on your Earth plane. We have witnessed, we have listened to excuses, and we have failed to see attitude change among those in power and in charge. It is those at the upper echelons of power in business, in industry, in government, who contribute the most in damage, while the masses who contribute the least feel disempowered to make improvement. We share how to change that balance, make those responsible, accountable, and empower the average person to hold them to account.

The ability for mankind to speak about their opinions and act on their inner strengths and beliefs is lacking in much of your population. We see that guidance is needed for those in need to find their way to their own personal power. There is much to consider for people on this journey to self and Self, and we say the first step is in sharing the knowing that each person has a Higher Self to access.

In living the creation of your own reality, you each contribute to overall change in the world. The shift of energy from negative to positive moves the balance, and change occurs. It is the way of the past and the way and hope for the future.

To all who share curiosity of yesterday, today, and tomorrow, they will find answers and more questions within these pages. To question more rather than to adopt what has been put in front of you as fact—this is the impact. To consider options and alternatives and not be accepting of all you are told without a query—we do not preach but rather we invite deeper exploration of fact.

To study this book, page by page, is the way as a quick read does not seem possible. To study this content becomes then a study of philosophy and physics, of metaphysics and religion, of astronomy and self-help, and further, the study of empowerment which enables all else. This is our greatest wish that your world's people become empowered and strong and take on the planetary repair now in desperate need of leadership. Do unto Earth; it's not too late, but we ask your people to "*get on with it.*"

We have much still to learn. Let's continue our talk.

We should like to point again to the wise ones of past times who circled their people and taught lessons of conscience and caring and working together to keep all people healthy and fed and educated.

We wish to say that moving ahead we speak of the need to think differently and act differently toward one another and your planet. When you understand this need, improvement comes.

What does it take, Pax, for people to understand this?

In order to reach the change needed to save Planet Earth, each inhabitant needs to be that change, yes? Be the change you want to see.

It is their journey to self that is needed, and specifically the journey to Higher Self. For most, they do not understand the difference and we are in place to show the way to put feet on the path to wellness of Self, and self. This is the lesson now for your people.

We speak of greening the planet and clearing pollution, but until your people have cleared their own clouds and purified their own thinking and living, they aren't likely to look further afield to do good.

We shall begin within, then work to with-out. Yes?

Yes.

We are here to show the way of change for Earth people, to revert to their history and their peaceful ways as taught once, and through this to find their way back on their journey to Self; the Higher Self. For Earth people to understand the difference between self and Self, their Higher Self, is a step toward understanding there is more to them and their daily lives than they imagined and brings the curiosity and need to learn more and grow more into what each can be. On this path comes wisdom and awareness of what is and what can and should be in life on Earth—this is our direction at this time.

Many people today feel disempowered to make change or to "be the change".

Yes, we say the attitude of, "Well, I can't make a difference," must stop.

It is for everyone to understand they can make a difference and it is up to them to act on this belief and share this belief with others who may be in doubt. Whatever the situation in the world where people are trying to be their best and do their best, it must be remembered that each person can make a difference.

When grouped together, of course, the crowd power takes on its own capabilities and much can be accomplished. Realize that the first few steps are the hardest and when they are taken, the snowball effect comes into play and the power of the people is felt.

Be aware that the power of the people begins with the power of one.

To clarify for our reader as we begin to talk about empowerment, what's the difference between *empowerment* and the *Higher Self*?

One keeps feet on floor, and one is a journey to inner wisdom—not even close.

Okay, good. We'll get to Higher Self; let's look first at empowerment.

The word empowerment indicates the empowering of a person, an inner strengthening and emboldening which enables that person to live their life to its best and attract that which serves him to his highest and best good.

This is a popular topic for us, especially now. Many people want to live their best lives and practice self-confidence—they want to know that they have a voice and something to say, and, most importantly, that they have the courage to use their voice, speak their truth, and follow it up with action.

Pax, because you are talking about empowerment in a book titled *Do Unto Earth*, I have a feeling that our empowerment has a much bigger purpose than what we currently understand in terms of its usefulness for our best-life or personal motivation.

What could be our future outlook if the majority of our world population got this message and became truly empowered?

The peace that comes to the globe is palpable and brings with it another type of world and lifestyle. Greed and corruption are things of the past. Errors in judgment are made in small ways that are corrected quietly and peace in the heart spreads to peace in the Universe.

When people look back on your civilization and on the wars and skirmishes and non-war conflicts around the globe, they will shake their heads and wonder how archaic that was and how people of this time could be so narrow-thinking and acting.

Narrow thinking will be our legacy; that is a shame.

Now you think world peace is a silly thing to think could actually be; not so. Remember to move in the direction of understanding that world peace will be. Feel it, it's palpable. Act like you are already there. Feel the feeling and spread the feeling and each do your part to bring peace into your lives and your environment.

I'd like to get your opinion on some debatable subject matter because it pertains to the images and awareness of world issues that we take into our minds and consciousness.

I'll give you an example: I became a vocal activist for animal welfare because I faced the reality of issues that are very hard to see and to know. My belief is that if animals have to go through such torturous lives and deaths, then at the very least, I will allow myself to know the truth of what is happening at the request and demand of humankind's whims and appetites. (Think of the fur industry where frightened foxes and tender chinchillas are electrocuted. Or, the way in which alligators are staked and skinned—often while still alive—because cutting their throats damages the valuable skin used for boots and handbags. Or, think of the wholesale slaughter of twenty-three million animals per day that occurs on our planet

just for food; a number that has greatly increased in the wealthier countries in recent years.)

When I became aware of these horrific truths, I became an activist and a voice for animals. This also naturally led me on a path to become an environmentalist and it helped prepare me for my part in the mission that we share. This awareness has formed my life's purpose in ways and depths.

On the flip side of all of that is the advice by some that one should not expose one's self to such "negativities", and that our goal should be to only envision and hold the images of what we want the world to be. For example, we should only hold positive thoughts and not seek to know those compartmentalized portions of life and the ways in which we get our consumer goods. While I believe in the practice of envisioning and focusing on the good, with tunnel vision we would have no environmentalists, humanitarians, or world-changers of any kind.

May you please speak to this and help to unpack our social/moral responsibility? And may you also speak to the beauty in living a life in purpose and on-purpose—if only we are aware and awake in the world?

Each person is empowered to change themselves and their world, some locally and some globally. Those temperamentally unsuited to strife and activism in person, many choose to write their concerns while others are suited to crowd speaking and crusading. Each has value.

In order to change what is felt unjust, one must know it; so burying head in sand does not contribute well. Awareness is one thing and moving forward with change while protecting one's self from inner hurt is possible. There can be crusading without immersing one's self in a scenario—levels of involvement exist, and each must choose theirs.

Knowledge is power.

In discussing empowerment, perhaps we should consider how dependency can be disempowering. For instance, receiving too much help and becoming dependent on outside resources dampens one's ability to know their potential and true power.

Would you concur and do you have wisdom to add on to this thought?

Of course it follows and the study of finding one's inner strengths has been much discussed.

As we have stated, all begins with believing the self is worthy, and knowledge of self in terms of wishes and wants and strengths and leanings and cravings as well as fears and phobias and disbelief and unwillingness to consider certain ideas are fence-posts along the pathway to inner strength or weakness. Each has the ability to choose.

Free will is limited only by self and the associated lack of trust in self.

No lack of self-empowerment should exist, but it does, and this reduces the availability of perceived choice.

All is possible when *trust in self* is in place.

Having touched on dependency, these lessons of trust in self and empowerment lead me to mention independency. I would like to point out that we are in an interesting time where many people are getting married much later in life as compared to generations past, and some don't get married at all, instead choosing to devote their time and passion to careers or purpose pursuits. What are your thoughts on this and is it okay to focus on our own spiritual development, talents, and passion-pursuits as a fully involved dedication?

You will not lead you wrong.

We are here to say that the nesting-syndrome practiced by many of your world will come to an end. There is to be a large event, taking place in the northern hemisphere, which will alleviate the need for this, and the many will change their habits.

Oh, do tell. What is this large event; this metamorphosis in the northern hemisphere?

What we see is single people and lots of them. We see professionals who have opted to remain true to their professions and their self-study and growth internally, and not combine their lives with partners and/or families and children. The new age of strong and single professionals begins now with the feeling that there is much work to do globally. The need to focus on it is too intense to share oneself with a relationship called marriage and the resulting offspring which take the focus away from world repair and interplanetary travel.

Follow your heart if you are one who has been feeling this pull and you will find your passion. This is key: passion and destiny come together most often and it is for you to recognize this and allow it into your lifestyle.

The best of the best comes from each person when they leave room in their lives for their light to shine brightly from within. This light is ignited when one does what one is put on Mother Earth to do: to create, to bring their gifts and talents to the forefront and shine their light onto the world. Think of it: your light can shine so brilliantly it will illuminate the world. So, recognize this and allow it to rise brightly and be the halo around yourself and your gifts to the world.

Of course, we both know that individuals can successfully follow their passions and purpose whether single, married, or married with children, but I get your point: people are feeling freer than ever to make that choice for themselves and to choose time and space to live their deep purpose.

We are here to speak with you now on the state of affairs in your world as it applies to self-preservation and self-motivation and self-empowerment: all very important topics to the people of your time. Now it is for you to realize that there is much work to be done on your planet and that all of these are needed by your people in order to begin and continue and complete the work necessary to ensure successful preservation of your lifestyle and your people.

You're not messing around here, are you Pax?

Empowerment should be much more than a genre of books, workshops, and seminars; it should be a collective philosophy. It should also be something we teach our children and should be as commonplace as learning about the alphabet, reading, mathematics, and walking and talking for that matter. Do you agree?

We say the reality of your need today to rise above what people consider their personal glass ceilings and break through by way of developing trust in personal power. This is the way of it.

It is for us to point out that while many have been raised in the belief that they can accomplish what they set their minds to, a great many have not, and further to that have been schooled in the belief that they should not aim too high. This is no way to instruct a child in the belief in Self. For those who don't subscribe to this philosophy, rather they believe that the sky is not even the limit, the stars and moon are theirs and more.

The likelihood that children born in your world today will live in another solar system or on another planet is to be considered. We have discussed that at your present rate of planetary destruction, you should be thinking of alternatives to call home. Given that this is the case, it is necessary to consider personal power and focus on its development within as a topic of study in school. We don't believe it receives sufficient focus.

Structurally, the school systems are in trouble, as is the human race: too much emphasis in the wrong places. Come on people, wake up and smell the failure of your systems.

As your children in school are taught reading, writing, and arithmetic, or variations on those to suit the times, these children must be taught belief in themselves, trust in their own abilities, and understanding that personal differences are to be explored and enjoyed, not treated as a reason to mock or exclude on the basis of color or economic status, dress, or language. Inclusivity and mining the depths of knowledge of each culture and language is the way to grow these children into trusting and self-empowered adults who view differences as strengths and interesting ideas to consider. *United Nations* of individuals as children are found in schools and their differences should be celebrated while drawing wisdom from the history of each culture. It is through this amalgamation of cultures that the cream raises to the top and the working together of all for the highest purpose becomes reality.

It is good that children are taught academics and sports and music, but please don't forget personal development, personal power, trust and belief in self, expanding consciousness, and those studies that instill in the young that they have unlimited capabilities and should know their imaginations can take them anywhere they want to go.

Pax, as we seek to evolve, where do we go from here?

We suggest that moving ahead with empowerment now is a good thing as most humanity lacks the strength of purpose required to become speakers for the planet at this time. We also wish to speak more on collective consciousness and the harnessing of that. While Universal Consciousness should also become a topic, it is the collective consciousness that helps people understand they do not stand alone in a protest.

Let's look at them both. This term might be self-explanatory, yet what do you wish to share about "collective consciousness"?

When we refer to collective or collected consciousness, it is to describe the critical mass of those who, when combining their thought powers to make a change, can do so with relative ease. It is the empowerment of these individuals to know that when they place their intention on an outcome, and together send their energies to that end, magic happens and, as we say, mountains may move.

It is power of the people in their unification behind a need and a creation of desired outcome. There is major change that can be made when group consciousness works to bend the spoons of what they see as wrong. This is a metaphor for the ability to send their energy, for good, and create the best possible outcome as intended.

What is Universal Consciousness and how can we access it?

This is Source energy, the Universal mind, the wisdom of the ages—all there to be accessed. Much like our wisdom and energy, as we have stated, it is there for the enlightened and anyone can access it. We channel together here and now, but others may also reach up to the Universal energy for their own learning. We do not restrict our wisdom nor does the Universal Consciousness restrict access to those seeking. It is the reason for being, to share, to be the resource and to carry the records of all that was and all that is, making this knowledge available in love to those who go within themselves in contemplation or meditation and seek to receive.

Excellent—consciousness is a resource pool that we can tap into for wisdom and empowerment.

Does consciousness have a tipping point, so to speak, whereby if x-number of people were to hold a belief/knowingness, then that wisdom or idea is virally spread through collective consciousness?

If tipping point means that it takes a specific number to activate the collective consciousness, then not so. The power of one is magnified by as many as are present and grows from there. Small beginnings may result in a growing of an idea and growing of the manifestations of these small ideas into global change.

Never underestimate the power of one voice.

You said: "We also wish to speak more on collective consciousness and the harnessing of that." Let's be sure to cover the harnessing part. How is collective consciousness harnessed?

Well, it is the case that it is the power of collected consciousness that is harnessed. When masses put their thoughts and minds onto a topic, combined with an intention, proverbial mountains may be moved. It is the raising of that energy to a level where the blending becomes the power and the holding of that energy in a place of intention for a common outcome gives it the teeth, the power, and the ability to make change. It is the way and it is too often overlooked by your people. Everyone has personal power and if it is magnified by themselves times the many others in the collective, amazing outcomes are created.

I'm now more accurately understanding what empowerment is and just how powerful and important it is. Our empowerment as individuals is our confidence in the idea that we can create change as individuals and that many empowered individuals together are power.

If you can dream it, you can do it, or it can be done.

Chapter Sixteen

Clearing Clouds (In Self and the World)

*I*n earlier conversations, you've tipped us off to the need for us to clear our own clouds before we can rise to our Higher Selves and/or affect greater change in the world around us. What exactly is clearing the clouds in self?

This is where the trust comes in. Just go toward it (your inner voice and higher calling) and do not listen to detractors who can dilute enthusiasm and change the course of one's feet along the pathway.

Who are the detractors who can dilute enthusiasm?

Family is often the strongest detractor for people who hear a higher calling. If it is not traditional it is not respected in many circles. Hogwash. Do not listen to this—if the world leaders who are untraditional—scientists, composers, and artists—listened to this drivel, where would your world be today?

Yes, this is true about the undermining of our dreams by one's own family, but *why* is this the case when family should be one's greatest supporters?

Unlike friends, family members will feel entitled to control the path of one of their own. If it does not meet with their approval or prescribed philosophy, it will be contradicted, and attempts made to change the trajectory.

Friends have more respect and will talk and guide and listen and offer thoughts and opinions, but with love. Not that family doesn't act out of love, it is usually the case but the need for conformity confuses their thinking and actions and results in enmity where there should be understanding: a sadness always.

Interesting, family members might have a need for conformity within the family beliefs and culture: I hadn't looked at it quite this way—this is helpful.

Allow faith in one's self to rule. "I rule" is the mantra. "I rule in my life." "I am number one"—"for if I do not develop myself to my full potential, how can I inspire others, children, family, students, etc. I must learn my full potential and find it." This is what makes a fulfilled person and one who contributes to society in the strongest way possible.

Each personality has their strengths and challenges, and it is for each to recognize this and begin the journey to Self, casting aside doubt and reaching for the stars and moon. Someone said, "Reach for the moon, then if you miss, you'll still land in the stars." We think this appropriate.

Do not be held back emotionally or mentally or physically. Trust in your Self and follow your heart.

As we strive to exercise our voice, to live in conscious creation, to act in bravery, and to trust in our own self and intuition, what else should we allow to drop away as we "clear the clouds" in our thinking as individuals in terms of our personal lives and interpersonal relationships?

Well this is a good thought and to each his own. When a goal is identified, whether it be personal or for the good of all, it will be felt, and anything entering the field of personal power that is detrimental to the achievement of that goal will be known, identified, and deflected.

To not allow in those roadblocks placed there by detractors, is the way. One must understand one's own personal power, trust in it to take them to the finish line and deflect interference where it is felt and seen. Much like a sports game, there are those propelling forward and those defending and blocking the intended goal, and only one will win. You choose which you will be.

We are here to say the time is now to understand that moving ahead in one's lifetime in happiness and abundance is dependent on living up to one's potential in one's heart. When a person does what they love, they love what they do, this makes for a happy and fulfilled life, which attracts abundance to the person as they are functioning at a high-level of vibration and attracting goodness unto themselves. Without all these components in place, when one or more is missing, a person is not fulfilled and therefore not completely happy: in this state there is consternation and an undercurrent of dissatisfaction leading to disharmony in the soul. This frazzles the life cord and causes it to vibrate to a lower-level, bringing disharmony and unhappiness to the person.

The long-term result is the person being unfulfilled and resentful of a life not well-lived, and resentful of others who they perceive are holding them back from their dreams by virtue of expectations placed on them for work, child raising, marriage requirements, geographic location, or other. It is a self-perpetuating situation causing one to spiral downward. Very destructive is this.

You got my attention with "life cord". What is the life cord?

Each of you comes into a lifetime with a plan, a blueprint, an agreement for what you bring and are to learn: this is your life as it is intended. We refer to the life cord as a visual so you can imagine if there is a kink in the cord, or an injury to the cord where it is made thin or burned or cut, that life interrupts and does not go according to divine plan. The plan is the agreement that the soul makes for its evolution through learning in the next lifetime chosen to live. Lessons are to be learned and taught through closeness with the people chosen as parents and family in each incarnation. To disturb this means to begin again in the next lifetime together, *if* this is the chosen life lesson to be learned and healed between them.

Can a person get to a point where the reasons that their soul originally chose another soul with which to journey—for instance a parent(s)—have been fulfilled, and they can now choose to cut off access to the person that continually harmed and sabotaged them? Basically, can there be a time when our soul-business is done with another who hurts us, and is there a best or correct way to officiate such a completion of soul-work, karma, or soul-travel together?

Our surprise at this question is coupled with a sadness for those who continue to accept less than deserved and consider it duty.

It is for your people to know they do not give away their power, and then in that place of being, find their own happiness or productivity.

To divest yourself from that which no longer serves you is the way, whether it be a person in the role of parent, or an old sock if it no longer contributes to your wellness and happiness and inner peace, especially if it does the opposite. If that sock has a hole in it or that parent rejects your being and refuses to accept you for who you are, then in aid of continuing your mental, spiritual, emotional, as well as physical good health, you may cut the cord and release yourself from the constant barrage of criticism and turmoil that contributes to your life. This is hardly a question of being polite or honoring another person: it is protecting your self and rising to the mission and purpose for this, your lifetime.

Why are you and what are you to become and contribute to your world today? Do you have the inner strength to make this journey and fulfill your reason for being? Will you take back your power, your inner strength of your own convictions? Or will you succumb to another's demands and shrink from the purpose you so dearly hold true and wish to commit to? In your vernacular we say it is a no-brainer. We support the truth of following one's heart and trusting in one's self—in this way, you will know the answers to these questions and make the choice that best serves you and your world to which you want to commit your powers.

The decision to sever the tie, cut the cord, is yours to make, each of you, and it is yours to return power to yourself and speak your truth in kindness. There is no one way or right way, there just is the way, and that is to go within to your heart and feel what is to be right for you. That you feel your soul journey together is complete comes from within you.

It may be that it is just this lifetime experience that terminates in a lesson for both sides and the soul journey continues to new lessons in the next time together. To not throw the baby out with the bath water is the way; as one lifetime of conflict is met with lessons, do not consider there is nothing more to be learned. This is a lesson for one needing to take back their power, and a lesson for the parent as well. Which one learns their lesson? Which one grows from it? Time tells all.

Aha! "Clearing clouds" is a practice in our empowerment. This has come full circle—you're good Pax!

It feels right to clear our clouds by speaking our truth in kindness and to take back our power from those who would attempt to undermine or disempower us. It also feels right to keep an open mind as it relates to these ties; perhaps the whole purpose of the relationship is to at last become empowered in one's own Self and to cut, *not the life cord*, but the giving-away of one's empowerment to another's expectations at the cost of the spiritual evolution of both people.

Thank you. This perspective is both freeing and beneficial.

And, I might as well ask about romantic and marital relationships too because there are

countless people who feel stuck in unfulfilling or tension-heavy relationships: how does one know when they should continue trying to make it work because they have soul-work to do together, and when should they exit the relationship in order to end the fighting and hurt?

It is the inner voice and inner feeling that tells this story. How does one react to the thought of staying versus leaving? This is the heart feeling and the cell reaction, not the intellectual thought that guides.

When the feeling of trepidation overwhelms the feeling of hopefulness, this is the signal that the end is come for this relationship.

That there may be soul-work left to do is not sufficient reason to remain if that seems overwhelming. The soul-work will remain for later in the lifetime or it can be taken on in the next meeting of souls together in another lifetime.

If you agree that we are ready to move on, let's discuss clearing clouds in our world powers, politicians, governments, and industry.

You have said that you would like to speak about industry money supporting politicians and the deregulation and lowering of standards in terms of environmental protection. When industry funds politicians, they do so to sway them to their benefit and monetary gain. What a vicious cycle it is.

As I see it, one solution would be to completely ban political campaign funding, period.

Instead, a new system could be instituted where each viable candidate gets the same allotment of funds to promote their message. This would eliminate the potential for such favors returned and the keeping-happy of corporate donors and industry supporters. Do you foresee this as a potential change in our government system, and an effort that the populations should focus our attention on?

Penelope, to the extent that your people have willingness to consider this question, it would be finding approval. However, the reality is inherent: greed and political aspirations overtaking where conscience once was.

I wonder if these individuals can become enlightened and inspired to change, or should it be our goal to unite to ultimately unseat them because their intentions are not able to evolve as fully as is needed in this generation?

Looking at the controlling powers at the very top of banking and industry, plus the many corrupt politicians in all levels and departments of government, is it "out with the old and in with the new", or should we attempt to raise them up in consciousness to do better?

Unseating them, yes, and do not anticipate this to become reality within this generation. This level of entitlement and control is not easily released. No amount of intention to fill their heads with what is good for mankind and the planet will likely result in contrition to the extent they change their ways. Ultimately, via attrition, they will be replaced, and new beginnings can be undertaken with new thinkers and those who see the big picture for your world renewal.

Yes, I suppose it will take some time to turn over all of the bad apples in the banking industries, government, and corporations.

Pax, you have said that we need to unite and stand up to the powers that be in industry and government, and that you would tell us the "how" and "when" and "why". I think we've covered the "why". Perhaps you can give us a look at the "how" and "when"—is it time to start discussing this here and now?

We do not speak of warring and overthrowing government here: we speak of education and information-sharing and teaching of better ways that do not harm the planet.

I've come to know that war is never what you advise; as you've said, the "peaceful warrior" is the way for peoples and countries to talk through our differences.

As far as the Tetris of our government structures, there is much to discuss. What do you wish to speak to first?

There must be solutions given and alternatives offered for the ways you see that are detrimental to your world. This applies to construction and industrial waste mis-management, fish farming and so many questionable decisions made that line the pockets of some and wreak havoc on resources.

We wish to discuss the ways in which your people have put their own needs above those of others, particularly in the corporate world and, shockingly, government. There is much lining of pockets for personal gain and little lining of food bowls for the poor. This will bring continued negativity and dark clouds to your world and focus must be placed there. There are also to be options given as solutions and direction for change.

It is to be noted that as powerful and corrupt leaders in your countries continue in power, your people have given away their individual power to make a difference for the better. Your citizens are to recognize two situations: one, those in power tend to be corrupt and wishing to build their own riches, and two, your people have given away their own power to reverse this and bring change to industry and government through higher expectations and using their votes in all ways to do so. This is the beginning of change. If you do not give support to a person or thing, it loses power. Act on this for a beginning, then continue to grow your power as change comes.

Advances will be experienced in all areas and it is noticeable that those in the greatest need of self-confidence remain lacking while those not lacking continue to advance. Why is that?

Those lacking confidence don't want to expose their insecurity; it's a symptom of our current era of artificiality.

Admitting that one is in need of a backbone is the first step and then allowing the fullness of time to pave the way for acquiring one, that is the way.

The people of your Earth are at a crossroads now but within just half a generation their new cross-roads puts this one in a diminished light: to move ahead in technology or to advance philosophy is a question. As the world of the future splits in two, it becomes apparent that the philosophers are gaining and surpassing the technicians. And this is the way of the future. Advancing on the discoveries between now and then is the way of thinkers and educators who believe that the peace not war stance is desirable. Adhering to this mantra becomes the need for many.

As we understand the need for many to release their former need to conquer and rule other nations, it becomes clear that the laying down of arms and the taking up of books and peace banners is difficult for some and impossible for others.

It is certainly impossible when one is missing a backbone. This is why our self-empowerment is so important, huh?

We ask for those affected to understand that there is great need for this as bullets whiz by and bombs explode, taking young lives along with them. It is unthinkable that this brutality and barbarism should continue. Look to the future and understand that the first rule of peace is: do no harm to others and treat them as you wish to be treated—that old golden rule says it all.

In ancient civilizations was the time of "greatness" revolving around attack and conquer. Some time passed before it became clear that speaking of differences and resolving them amicably, not fighting, is the civilized way of the more highly evolved to reconcile differences.

In some countries there will never be a wide distance between the need to invade and conquer and the actual doing of same. Otherwise, the remainder of the world understands the benefit of speaking and bargaining and understanding the needs of each other and working through turmoil, allowing it to settle into peaceful accord is the highest ability there is, so that all parties are pleased with their lot, this is the gift.

Take no prisoners. Take no arms against others. Take only the wants and needs of others into account when attempting to resolve differences—this is the way for peace to reign and mankind to flourish.

You have been making a very straightforward point, and that is that our government leadership is directly tied to our success in saving our planet

and healing our environmental crisis. And yet, your even greater and more profound point is that in order to clear the clouds of government we must first clear our own clouds and activate our individual personal power in addition to acting on our collective responsibility to be empowered. Am I getting this right?

Yes.

What we wish to speak of now is the way in which the greening of your planet must go together with the greening (enlightening) of your Earth's people in that they look toward expanding their vision to include seeing their higher capacity, their higher probability for success when they come from a place of love within themselves, and this is how they treat all people and places and things.

We are here now to discuss the way that your Earth people disinherit their attachment to your Mother Earth. In this attitude they feel no responsibility for her care and feeding. How is it that they can look the other way while casting about plastics and caring little for where it all ends up in your landfills?

Now we draw the parallel between the raising of human consciousness with the resulting improvement in the life and lifestyles of your people. Do you see the need for life and liberty and freedom for all? Do you look at the way countries and cities are not treating people as equals? Where is it written that the mighty and rich may run roughshod over the more hard-pressed for survival and meeker citizens they pass on the roadways? This is not the way to move forward in harmony among your people.

There are places in your countries where people of color have been persecuted, and not popular are people of some religions and people from countries other than those powerful and thinking they are the greatest. This tyranny is to cease, now, and if it does not there will be chaos. Look to world history in the last century alone to show how this comes to be when those who see it do not speak up.

It is a dangerous situation beginning now to repeat.

You are pleading with us to remember the 1940s and earlier political upheavals, aren't you? (The tyranny of the Nazis from that era comes to mind, as does present-day communism in Russia, North Korea, and elsewhere.)

Lifting our hearts and minds to what your people can contribute and how your abilities grow, we share that it will represent two steps forward and one step back, into the future, or even worse if your course of sociopathic leadership in politics is not neutralized.

This is serious.

We wish to bring people to the knowing that they can create peace and harmony in their lives, in their families, in their workplaces, and in your cities and your world if all will think this way.

Like pebbles into the pond creating ripples of peace, these intentions will transmit to the dark places and illuminate what is there for all to see.

Let there be light—be the light—sweep away the darkness.

The Russian government claims that they now have an intercontinental nuclear strike weapon that can travel twenty-seven times the speed of sound. Is this one of those foreboding concerns of our time?

Where is proof and where does the inflated truth run over into the not so truth side of reality? Well now, we say this is a media frenzy and much ado about nothing. There is little truth and no proof and therefore no need to look further.

What science in this country can accomplish is strong and quite influential and impressive, but what this country sets out to do is conquer and vanquish and strong-arm others to the extent that they shoot themselves in the proverbial foot at times for entering into research and development with bad intentions. The Universe does not like this and support for their ongoing success is not there.

Do not wait for the other shoe to drop.

Speaking further on the goal of neutralizing "sociopathic leadership", I'll cut to the chase:

which countries are in most urgent need of leadership-from-the-top reform, and why?

One word fits all: corruption. European and Asian countries, South American countries, Russia, China, and who is considered the one to manage and set a good example for all? The USA, which is in perhaps the weakest position of all given the explosive actions of your politicians, again. Allowing the actions to be taken that place all in fear—we question the need and there is no reason for this complacency.

It is a sad situation that portends more sadness to come before the sun rises over the lands and peace reigns. There will be upheavals and overthrows and election losses that make the minds of many hurt for trying to explain and understand the trajectory of current politics on your soil. It is a conundrum— these next many turns of your Earth planet, and when it is making sense once again, it will be well into your future.

We wish to say that your world is in turmoil and chaos now politically. There is to be repercussion and it will be felt as ripples on the water for some time—escalation occurs, and lives are lost.

It is sadness to the Universe, and we speak of ripples on the water—these ripples now extend beyond the galaxy and reinforce the view of your interstellar friends that your planet is set on a course of self-destruction, immolation.

That *is* very sad.

Here in the United States, we have much division between our political parties. Citizens are nearly divided down the middle and both sides have no interest in seeing the other's perspective; both believe that they are in the right. You could say it's a cold civil war.

It is our wish that your people spend more time accessing their own Higher Selves to rewire their ways of being. Too often there are sheep following where there should be rams leading. Those currently leading your world powers are doing not a good job of it. In your soon time will be upheaval and a not pleasant experience for many, but it will result in greater input by the people in the make-up and running of governments.

It is time now to know that the days and decades of sitting back and watching corruption unfold, without defiance from the people, is over. There must be choices made and actions taken to remove from world power those who are leading your people into disarray on the world stage.

The time is now to take your power back, all of you, and stand up for what is right. Reversal of fortunes for those in power and raking in the many big moneys for their own pocket lining—this is underway and must come to the forefront of your news as a happening thing and be stopped.

How do you walk through each day knowing corruption is and corruption spreads and you have no recourse? Of course you do: stand up and say you do, then follow your hearts and move into the next stage of cleanup.

It begins with you.

Sometimes governmental lies and industry corruption can feel overwhelming. You said that change comes as we continue to grow our powers and abilities. What powers will we develop that will turn the imbalance of power from the government and industry giants to the people?

There are now those who understand that change comes—change in the way of implementation of the new order. This means that those who sit back and take from your world will have slim pickings and those who step up and give will be the receivers. Is this as it should be? We think so.

Penelope, the time comes for whose role it is to improve the lives of those around them to be the recipients of improvements and those who diminished their world will be diminished in the eyes and hearts and minds of those who see truth.

Coming soon, *all peoples will see truth and work on instinct*—much more than in recent generations of your civilization. In past civilizations this was the case, but intuition and intuitive action has diminished to the point of extinction almost in the masses. For those with the gift, they know the truth is out there and it soon becomes close to all and visible.

Bringing forward the gifts of telepathic communication improves life and changes life to the degree that it is all but unrecognizable. Think on it: that you can understand the mind and wishes of someone who needs not speak the words. What can be hidden away? The truth *is* out there, out there in the ethers for all to access. That is the meaning, don't you know?

This will separate the wheat from the chaff, as they say.

Going forward in business and politics will be quite a different affair. Think on it: what can be hidden or buried or not discussed? What truth can be avoided and what untruths covered? It is to be the greatest change that your world has seen in a very long time.

Moving into this era will happen quite naturally as a shift continues in your earthlings who are open to their spirituality and their gifts and talents regarding communication: the unspoken variety.

Oh, my goodness, Pax: it's now becoming apparent as to why it is imperative for us to seek our spiritual development and our innate abilities—it's the way to truth, light, and peace.

It happens seamlessly until one day it is observed that lies and untruths are recognized for what they are, and the "wool" can no longer be easily pulled over the proverbial eyes of society. People just become aware that they know or understand things and live their lives more acutely. It is a beautiful thing to see develop.

Those who are slow coming to this place in their lives will understand that time will unfold as it should, and they too will come to a time and place where the ability materializes. There is no specified timeframe for this other than to say that those who are further along on their spiritual paths will recognize it in themselves sooner and be able to counsel others as to its imminent arrival for them.

Wow.

And, what does "doing business" look like in this new era?

Transparency is how it looks. As we have spoken, there is no hiding of thoughts and intentions. Think of this and smile—those who purport to be well-intentioned are seen through the microscope of intuition and transparency and must either change their ways or become a fringe player on the stage of life. Honesty and idealism prevail.

This is revolutionary.

Penelope, this is the time of all times for those who begin to experience this gift, and gift it is.

Clearly, this is the change responsible for much greater future changes in your world as infidelity and greed and fraudulent actions make way for transparency. Think of that.

Our way is to advise you of what is to come, to fortify you for the experience. Positive and more highly evolved behaviors result and the greater steps toward harmony on your planet to be taken—go now and contemplate this change for it is a significant one for your time.

Again, we say look to the past for your future. These civilizations of long ago who routinely communicated this way will show you the way and there are messengers here now, of course, watching and readying for the new age.

It is poised to begin.

We speak of transparency in all, and this comes within a few generations.

As the mindset of your people changes to good and acceptance and love and honesty, so does your means of communication leave the written and spoken word much of the time and become telepathic thought communication.

Allowing for the fact that nothing can be hidden when thoughts are read, clarity and honesty become the norm. Other thoughts that are dark-energy-sourced or nefarious are instantly known as your people have reached a level of intuitiveness meaning nothing is hidden.

It shifts behaviors immensely.

$$\bullet \bullet\bullet \infty \bullet\bullet \bullet$$

About the Author and Channeler

*P*enelope Jean Hayes is a new consciousness author, television personality, and speaker. She has appeared on-camera hundreds of times as an expert guest on programs including *Dr. Phil*, *ABC News*, as well as international news specials and telecasts. She is the foremost leader in the field of contagious and osmotic energy known as Viralenology, founder of the Viral Energy Institute, and author of the book *The Magic of Viral Energy: An Ancient Key to Happiness, Empowerment, and Purpose.*

Carole Serene Borgens channels Pax, the Divine Wisdom Source. Carole is a former nurse and longtime student of metaphysics. She has been channeling Spirit since the early 1990s when she was chosen by Pax and given the title "Spirit Messenger". Carole continues to write and provide in-person and remote sessions for clients around the globe, and she refers to her gift of channeling as "the greatest blessing in my life."

Of this trio, Pax says, "A good team we three."

www.PaxWisdom.com
www.PenelopeJeanHayes.com
www.CaroleSereneBorgens.com